Amoretti

ALSO BY JOHN PURSER
and published by Aquila

THE COUNTING STICK

A SHARE OF THE WIND

AMORETTI
JOHN PURSER

AQUILA : ISLE OF SKYE

BRITISH LIBRARY CIP DATA

Purser, John
Amoretti.
I.Title
821'.914 PR6066.U'/

ISBN 0-7275-0353-7
ISBN 0-7275-0354-5 Pbk
ISBN 0-7275-0355-3 limited signed ed.

First published 1985 by
AQUILA PUBLISHING COMPANY
an imprint of
Johnston Green Publishing (UK) Ltd
P.O. Box 1, Portree, Isle of Skye, Scotland IV51 9BT

CONTENTS

AMORETTI

I

There was no kind of hunting when we two
sighted each other – perhaps I stared, maybe
you turned your head, and as our bodies drew
together as a mare and stallion free
at last in the one field we nuzzled cheeks
breathing each other's breath; or as the sea
nudging explores its own flood-tide and seeks
new land above familiar marks, and talks
among strange rocks and crevices, or speaks
words of enticement, so did we in walks
along the edge of our own shores – till brave
enough to step where custom baulks
and, as sea-horses playing in a wave,
to prance and tumble in the joy its breaking gave.

II

That winter day my feelings were still numb
as we took time together on the hill,
followed by earnest hungry sheep, whose dumb
demand and shuffling feet in snow were still
behind us after half a mile, while we
laughed winter laughs and chased them back until
they guessed we were of some strange pedigree
anxious to be alone; yet thanks to you
not lonely, as we slithered to a tree
and I then held you so you'd have the view
over my shoulder of the fields below
where, puzzled, the sheep watched our love renew
the teasing innocence of long ago
fooling and kissing in the melting snow.

III

When we were young
we were not afraid
to walk barefoot in wet grass at midnight
stroking our cheeks with bog cotton or the edge of a feather:

but now we do all these things
and use our lips and eyelashes
as well.

When we were young
we would run down hills
till our feet thumped the breath out of us
and our laughter came in gasps:

but now, what with running and laughing and kissing,
we are twice as breathless and when we run
we have each other harnessed round the waist
and our hips touch.

When we were young
we were not afraid
to make nests for ourselves in dead bracken protected by
arches of brambles:
but we did not make love in their shelter
in the spring gales as we do now, and you handle your skirt
with even less modesty than you did as a girl.

I can see the way this is leading us:
you loving me and me loving you
is making us younger than anyone has ever been before
except for Adam and Eve:

But we have the fun
of knowing all about it
and when we pluck figs
we leave the fig leaves on the trees.

IV

Where you sleep now I travel to in mind,
from six miles high fancying we pass your dreams
under our wings in the jet stream of night:
below, spark ribbons leading to a town
that gathers like a galaxy, or the one light
from a ranch attic starring the dark pasture,
tip all my senses over to the ground
gathering dreams from where they might float free
to where you sleep and have reality.

V

I write this poem with a heart of stone,
scratching Ben Sgriol, or a slip of it from
the cairn, having no paper and no pen
but the smooth heart-shaped stone you gave to me –
from a long shore an ocean wide away –
which streaks its heart-dust on the mica-schist.
Below green sphagnum, cushioning a spring,
seeps to a lochan on to slake the sea
where – if these stones should slip into the stream
and nudge past pools to where the limbs of land
spread for an estuary – our hearts will be
tumbled and fussed, and all my metaphors
will loosen their old troubles in the waves
of true events shouting and shingling on the shores.

VI

Remember, love, before you blame us both,
the high-bridged stream with fallen trees below
where you, brushing the damp furze from your face
returning sodden from the autumn woods,
the stream a torrent, now fancied its force
uprooting all that wreckage in the hour
we were gone, knowing it was not so.
In other places you have said the tide
might swoop us past the bridge and leave us slack
in dead water, but the sea will turn
this way swooping again and seeming never tired
of its old games, just as among the oaks
we saw a daft November butterfly
still dodging drips and leaving through the damp
a white trail flickering with some mad delight
of nature, natural to all, to us also.

VII

Sometimes I seem a wind about your house
that thumps at gables and through gaps of doors
sneaks in with troubled gusts where a slim mouse
runs furtive between hidey-holes on floors
fanned by a searching draught. Noisy outside,
or silent, but within, I give you cause
to fear turmoil should you at last decide
to air the house when winter might prevail.
But, thrust by a wild element denied
too long till you first loved me in a gale,
and troubling still to pin the leaves you wreathe
round old memorials, you must not quail —
for all the worrying that the winds bequeathe
is spent to keep alive the air we breathe.

VIII

I asked what you would like, and when you said
'something I'd made myself and made for you',
daft notions, twitterings of a poem or two,
hopped into sight, cheeky as birds with heads
cock-eyed for bacon rinds and praise: but who
am I to fetch an aviary to your lawn,
who cannot stand the noise now it's near dawn
and one eye open's all that I can do
after a night of study full of yawns
as dumb as a sick budgie – but don't take
my bird-seed from me yet since, for your sake,
I'll chirp a chirrup for when you were born,
and though my gift for song's but half awake,
don't you forget you have the gift of everything I make.

IX

In the brown Kelvin
a duck and drake struggle after rain;
missing the one eddy that curls up to the bank
they hold together
in the ominous ripple of flood water.
But, giving way, she looks down river
as she's swept towards the weir,
so he gives in as well.
Just as I start to fear for them
with white-barred flashes
they both take to air.

And now at night twelve eider –
thirteen – push into the ebb
at Hungerford
while we lean on a granite balustrade
and kiss under a hat and an umbrella's slant.
A distant trumpet busks from the far bank
across reflections,
and the ducks
dip and snuffle in the dark water
billowing with mud.

It should be nothing to us
that these plump feathered preeners
stay afloat – but still, I squeeze
the swell that marks your hip
under the warm fabric of your coat.

X

that time we huddled in the heather hills
so full of laughter as we fought to shield
each the other each from coming rain,
and rolling over on the springing stems
soaked our backs and faces and our coats
got stuck all over with dry pollen grains
and when we had to pluck and each brush down
the other's clothing – such gentle pressure
of your breasts under your coat –

do you remember how our discretion long ago,
seemed innocent of wrong? – and still seems so.

XI

Standing together in the clean night air
you watched the sea – we could just hear
the flood tide lapping – but I watched your hair,
dark, shining, slipped behind your ear
like water on its way round a smooth stone:
you seemed to have been flowing everywhere
in my best dreams – and then that night
how innocently we did not sleep alone
but clung kindly together – do you recall
when you undressed in the soft candlelight
I watched your shadow lapping on the wall?
Next day, not certain this was the real world,
I ran my fingers gently over all
the eddies in the sheets where you had curled.

XII

Now there are no misgivings we can give
and all those others who were drifting by
like mist about the rose in its green hedge
moist and insinuate, try
as they may, cannot evermore allege
it has no blossom save in a clear sky,
or spurn its offering as no true gift
because it's wild: for though we're on the edge
of winter, here's the uncultured day
still coloured by its rose and bees still fly
for fodder in its flowers, and the drift
of all that doubting damp surmise
has passed and leaves us only with the play
of light in ours to give to others' eyes.

XIII

I watched you garden under a dark sky
when cold winter horizontal light
ruffled the crumbled soil and crept round clods
discovering with huge shadows a late fly
or tumbling beetle, busy until night
burying a limp shrew where the brown pods
of broken beans lay flattened in the earth
by piled potato shaws all soft with blight;
and wondered how, in such a sullen time,
you dug tenacious, certain of the worth
of what you did and planting in despite
of all that loss, till the plants climbed
where your love sheltered the young growing part
in the old sheltered garden of the heart.

ARCHIE

From the blue boat with double prow
we lift the spilling fish-box to the rocks
to clean and fillet; as my knife edge grinds
against the spine, the head lifts
and the mouth forms to an 'O'
silent, before the air sac
breaches with a sigh.

Archie, who can't well speak
the daft thoughts in his mind,
watches, shifting weight
from leg to leg, like an old gull,
though now they scream about us
for their share of heads and guts
and rich fawn-coloured livers — I recall
a man at Mallaig guiding fish
in a receiving tank from the great tear-drop nets;
fighting the gulls with his affectionate roar
and sweep of arm, useless
to stop them perching on his head
or burying the fish beyond his grasp
under a plethora of wings.

Archie, given a chance,
will take all that he can —
from a good sharing of the catch
to cuddles with some scared embarassed wife.
Frustrated, his abuse echoes off outcrops
of the rock, is heard in every home.

But they tolerate his protest — he is more
than tolerated -- understood to be
as necessary as the gulls themselves,
for who knows but one day
his strange, half-innocent brain
will lead them, like the seabirds,
to a place where the heart's fish
are gathered to the shore so plentiful
that the wild combat, laughter and white wings
will fill his isolation with their love
and silence all the protest of his mind.

NASHAWENA

Here in the New World, still so new to me,
something familiar in the unkept track,
the half-forgotten spring, the smell of sea
or weathered porch – the gentle amity
of friends, considerate; brings welcome back
things I had feared long lost; though, being found
only half credited – as the muffled sound
of a bell-buoy lurching distantly
in fog. But though we're all on shifting ground
this island's rooted in mysterious sand,
as though the amaranth or the untouched tree
of Eden here might grow, as so do we,
discovering in what once was Prospero's land
our own youth catching us by heart and hand.

OUT OF SEASON

Under a grey wild sky wild roses toss
– husk hazel, rattling holly, twitch of birch –
at the broad stepping stones no one can cross
– drowned alder, splitting willow, creak of pine –

and you and I, walking above the cliff
in the wide draught of the atlantic air,
release our hands to go more safely there
– buzzards are plentiful and rabbits scarce –

so hurry home and coorie by the hearth
– quick birch, hot ash, green elder, steady rowan –
we'll kindle logs when we've stripped off the moss
and save the year, in bed, from total loss.

TO A LARK

Flickering bars of white and a green-grey
that flashes under-over-under-wing,
two larks in mock-fight mating
tumble each other over in the air
like balls of dead grass scattering in a gale.
Then one escapes and waiting for a while
grows disappointed and sets up
chirping attractions for a huffy mate.

Don't worry. Soon your more celebrated songs
will be woven like a spell to keep a nest,
a matted egg-filled hollow in the ground,
hidden – wrapped round about
in miles of tangled sound.

SKYLARK

who can unstitch a stretch of sky
and with the same song seam it up again,
or tirl the air and needle into notes
a trillion tiny ear-drum taps
with threaded light that makes my eyes,
hereditary, sneeze, and turn to ground
among the labouring insects
beetling balls of dung:

when you fly free and I'm left cutting peat
against a winter half a year away,
remembering at the end of Eden man
was given what would root him to the spot –
a spancelling spade –
I raise my hat and yield the gods a grin
as proof that all creation's crazy made.

TO HIS FAMILY, IN MEMORY OF WILLIAM ANGEL

What small thing has gone to ground this day;
leaf, rabbit, shrew or blackbird, pressed to clay
at the field's edge where the long clamps of straw
preserve the root crops by the graveyard wall,
each of its kind forgotten?
                                        But let this memorial
recall for him your gentle thought; to spread
a leaf and feel its veins, or tuck the head
of a hurt blackbird close under your jaw
as though under a wing, or let a shrew
run from the rubbish right over your shoe
quite unmolested, or to help once more
the rabbit find its burrow from the gun –
for such as these could not have killed your son.

MESSAGE

I did not
study beauty in a stall.
She took me by surprise.
In yellow asphodel:
in the jigsaw sutures
of a red deer's skull.
Today she's a person.
She wears
let's say a beret –
without solemnity.
She has come over high snows,
shivers a little.
I am in love with her already.

She sees that;
and sets up a theatre
in a grassy place
under heavy green boughs.
She enters from the wings
from between the dark trunks of trees.
No beret.
No clothes.
She is very old, very – well . .
beautiful.
Often loved.
She says her first speech
without sound,
but anyone could tell that she was saying
'Get out . . please get out . . just please get out.'

SLEEPERS

The night train
draws perspectives,
narrowing lines;
the wheels and bogies
tug me
like old age
my jacket hangs uneasy,
makes a shift
to shake my creases out
and hopes to fit itself
for others when I'm gone

. . . . . .

Did a girl come to that window
brush her hair
into a train of thoughts
as like as sad as like
as mine? . .

. . . . . .

the window glass now shows me
only me
my light my mirror.

. . . . . .

damp sheep and cattle
eating through the night –
full river, flooded field –
and up before the dogs,
a farmhouse child
lights up a skylight
in an attic room . .

. . . . . .

Leadhills.
Yellow square
and orange pool.
White slit. Pinhole.
Older already
she kisses him goodbye
sees him
slip north
into perspective.

Going south
the lines
are narrowing too.

NEAR DRINAN

A cow lies on the shore, her fall
full sixty feet from the jurassic cliffs
wooded and shrubby to the very edge.
Did the eye deceive her, or the foot –
what thought went through her heavy bony head,
what attempt to right herself as she fell?
The impact threw her excrement
clean from her bowel across a nearby rock.

Not half a mile from here's the Soldier's Point.
Returning from a long-forgotten war,
some friendly boat put him ashore
to find his last miles before darkness fell.
Did he stray to a cliff path
in inquisitive recognition, nearing home?
What trick of evening tangled his eye
in shadows, dropping him in a void:
did he lie thus, his lower jaw smashed sideways,
teeth awry, flies feeding in his deaf ears?

Everything here is smashed – shells, fish-box,
even rock. Between the indecision
of air and land and sea there is no burial
but rotting or floating off on full-moon tide.
In the old graveyard rowans keep the dead
docile with their shush of leaves. Here,
just half way up a steep cliff band of lime,
a primrose flowers. Water falls
incessantly – a drip catching its petals;
every time it dips and sheds the drop
and springs back up, drip after drip
until my neck is sore from watching it.

But as I drop my eyes the boulders swim
and my feet fumble for a steady place
as though delight had led me out of bounds
and my true study here
was these sad unparticular remains.

IN THE MANUSCRIPT ROOM OF A LIBRARY

Everything's a tree:
the curl of paper
the parquet floor
the desk-grain and the doorway
the catalogue cabinet's of wood
the hat-rack and the roof.
The sounds are trees :
chairs creak
leaves rustle
someone sighs
now and then one whispers
as the keeper, sheltering, bows
over a query.

Readers search like grubs
under the bark of books
shedding skin and hair:
a little draught
lifts wisps
from an old lady's chevelure
strayed from its loosening knot:
fingers rub foreheads
there is a scratch of pens
of branch and twig
scrabbling to set free
the deep concentric memory in the tree.

NOVEMBER FROM THE CLACH RATHAD

The Canna lighthouse, smearing out the sky
of soft grey half way indigo,
talks to Tex Geddes on the coast of Rhum,
his masthead light now making steady north
for Soay harbour on a full flood tide:
a car – just headlamps on a hill –
plunges from skyline down to Tarskavaig,
and a daft dog in Drinan barks
at the sudden shadow of a black cow's bulk;
a blackbird stutters and a snipe
startles along the shadowed ditch.
It is the time when searches are abandoned,
when the doe rabbit I stunned against a stone
shivers suddenly long past her death;
and the tilted landscape,
like a capsized sail, dips into the sea
of northern latitude so deep in indigo
it seems we'll never right ourselves
before Orion swings into the dark
certain to hunt us down.

INTERIOR

My room is decked with skulls:
an old ram jutting from the wall
without opponent; a cow that fell
to a rough rock shore;
a little goat that died in Italy
bearing her first kid.

My room is decked with green:
the fossil antlers of an elk festooned
with ivy; the mirror ivied – by the wall
a slender upstart tree
and grey Atlantic seal, baring his teeth,
a sprout of holly prospering in his snout.

Sound-sensitive is my room –
to hissing logs and hiss of pressure lamp,
or old cracked cello's sudden groan inside its case,
or my tempestuous daughter fluting air
for goats to dance to.

My room has its disturbances and fears:
the gannet's beak that I could never close;
the tiny theatre, ivy-overgrown;
the minute scream from some strange agony
far inside the fire.

This is Christmas eve. We sit alone.
The candles, tinsel, jigsaw half-undone.
Later, I watched her torch-beam on the moor
dart to a neighbour's, but from time to time
point back to pick me out – my arms outstretched
behind the gate to give a reassurance, held
only for its own sake – as it must be,
since there's such scant assurance in reality.

BOTTICELLI TO VENUS

This is our second childhood – not that age
has played the fool with us, but we have played
with the delight of children who engage
delight with neither fear nor loss. We've made
fools of dials and calendars, held court
in the long grass, the scythe and spade
have not troubled us, it's been our sport
to geld old Time and drop his genitals, maimed,
into the sea –

and look, I see you step
naked ashore; frank, touching, unashamed,
fresh from the scallop in the willow skep
through whose old uprights of despair and rage
I've woven hope, so men might catch and sow
the seeds of oceans – but where people grow.

GRANIA TO DIARMUID

Cast no more unbroken bread;
since he put his arms around me,
his hands pressed to my stomach,
since I thrust your knife into your own thigh
and you made me withdraw it to my shame,
let our token tomorrow be scattered crumbs,
crushed husks, the milled grain:
I have needed you beyond bearing;
as blood flowers in snowflakes I am torn
by the red rose and the white rose of your flesh.

TO BE SUNG IN ORBIT

What if my sounds have no sound
but the slip of water on glass
or of threads spinning round
the spinner earth where they pass
beyond the hearing of all, what then?

shall I ripple your view of the stars,
shout out defiance for long;
or cocoon the whole half-sleeping world
in a spinning song?

THE SONG OF THE GHOST

As I walked lonely by the river side
I felt the presence of someone who'd died
and wondered how I heard his call
against the wind and the waterfall.

He said he wandered where he'd lost his child
playing with water when both were wild;
he never heard his own child call
against the wind and the waterfall.

And then he whispered to me his name
and said my time had come to share the same,
for I had heard his shadow call
against the wind and the waterfall.

And now he's drawn me to his side,
the name he named me with can't be denied
by those who hear my shadow call
against the wind and the waterfall.

(Air: *The Song of the Ghost*)

FOR KIRSTEN MacLEOD ON HER FOURTEENTH BIRTHDAY

Fourteen's an age for sonneteers and you:—
so, to clean sweep the world we'll make a cloud
out of the grains of dust and count them too
and find if Archimedes has allowed
that gold can dance and dross can settle down —
for where's the joy in judging every crown
by dipping the world's particles in a pan
to measure up the mischieve that's in man:
besides, though I shall truly count my lines,
you'll tip fourteen for better measure still
and sweep beyond the folly that confines
my old ideas, intending to fulfil
more hopes than I remember — though I trust
that I will catch their sunlight in the dust.

FOR IVAN M****

I've an idea that fourteen lines of verse
make up a sonnet, not a birthday ode,
and, for a young man, should be fresh and terse
or preferably in computer code.
But fourteen years bring fourteen lines to mind
and, since you're learning French and German too
and speak so pleasantly, no doubt you'll find
a little room for English to wish you
a happy birthday – and accept these signs
from the brain's circuitry as a slim clue
to thoughts beyond computing, and designs
broad as affections; though, as my end nears,
I know I'll never fill my fourteen lines
with half the grace that you have filled the years.

TO ANDREW HOOK ON THE OCCASION OF HIS FIFTIETH BIRTHDAY

Andrew, a fisherman of men (of girls
No more, dear Judith, than belongs in trust to
Departmental heads), has cast across the
River of their minds beyond the swirls of
Eddying ignorance and the sharp gusts of
Wilfulness and, with but little loss,

Hooking the line of history to his lure
Offered to lurkers in the dark, has struck
Often the jaw of truth, but made the cure with
Kindness and returned the fish still vibrant at their luck.

ONE IRISHMAN TO ANOTHER

Ah, Bishop Berkeley, 'twill do you no harm
spilling beer on your Vision while raising my arm
to stifle a yawn – 'twas the hop, not the leap
of your tough mental games, that put me to sleep.
Now, if I get you right, I imagine the beer –
or put it this way, the beer's an idea
in my head – I agree – but if it was here
before it was there in the glass I'm not clear
as to how it has passed from my thought to my pleasure
without catalysts like some malt and that treasure
of flowers, the hop – though I tell you bell heather
will certainly do just as well: what a blether
you are Bishop Berkeley – I'm sure that the port
or tar-water you drank did just as it ought
to and if, Bishop Berkeley, 'tis all in my head
not Berkeley but beer'll blur my Vision instead.

AFTER–DINNER GRACE IN MONOMETERS, FOR TWO ONLY.

Take care
to spare
the heart
in part
at least
from priest
and prayer;
and share
the love
that dove
and cross
(they'd toss
a twig
or fig-
leaf on
our fon-
dling fights
these nights)
would claim.
A game
with nak-
ed stakes
is not
for rot-
ten roots
but shoots
and spears.
Though fears
beset
you, yet
please say
we may
succumb —
a crumb
won't feed

the seed
of lust,
and dust
to dust's
a must-
y creed
to feed
upon —
a mon-
ument
to spent
endeav-
ours nev-
er cast
to last.
But see;
I'll be
your priest:
at least
you'll know
that though
you fear
to hear
what's true,
if you
confess
I'll bless
your eyes,
your thighs,
your lips,
your slips
from grace,
embrace
the place
you know
I go
for most.

Oh host-
ess best
divest-
ed, share
my prayer:
and ans-
wering dance
this dance –
and dance,
entrancing, darling dancing dancer,
dance!

THE RINGER DOYLE

Oh come all ye idle browsers
and listen to my song
of a road-mender from Annamoe
where Laurence Sterne a long
time ago so nearly drowned
by the ground where presidents belong –
a throng of them did there reside
most undeservingly beside
The Ringer Doyle.

He had a pair of roomy trousers
and an ear-ring, gold and round;
you could find him around Roundwood
keeping dirt roads sound
and good to let mankind pass by –
his beady eye would always hound
you round well on the other side:
you wouldn't pass too close beside
The Ringer Doyle.

He was the best of tea carousers;
he brewed it in the ditch
each hour – his fires were quite a feat
in rain – the tea was pitch-
black, sweet, but sour with tanin taste;
and without haste his brush would twitch
and switch at ruts: – a bumpy ride
for all those who passed beside
The Ringer Doyle.

For political rabble-rousers
he never had respect,
and any call to action he
was certain to reject;
he'd see that all the evidence
that presidents select
for their elections was belied
when they would not stop beside
The Ringer Doyle.

Now the world is full of grousers:
when they reach the pearly gate
with their catalogues of woes
and repentance on a plate
who knows but that the Saint
will thus acquaint them of their fate:—
"It is too late! I have decide-
d I'll put none of you beside
The Ringer Doyle."

So harken to me now sirs:
this little rhyme should show
that thoughtful idleness and cease-
less efforts to go slow
give peace promotion in the soul,
and on the whole that's good; but know
that though you've idle lived and died
you could never stand beside
The Ringer Doyle.